Do You Speak Lease?

Finding & Negotiating Your Own Commercial Space

By: Lynn Drake

Do You Speak Lease?

Finding & Negotiating Your Own Commercial Space

What Others Are Saying About This Book:

Rod Santomassimo, Founder and President of the Massimo Group

Lynn's book provides keen insight into the world of commercial real estate leasing. Do You Speak Lease clearly defines each step in the process of finding and leasing office, industrial and retail space so it can be easily applied by novices and seasoned professionals alike, assisting the reader in successfully navigating a commercial real estate lease transaction.

Debra Lee Stevens, CCIM Principle of The Stevens Group

If you have leased space in the past 7-8 years, or never done a lease, renewal, expansion, termination or sublease: Read This Guide!

Lynn Drake's Tutorial is excellent. Listen to every word. Read and then Re-read. For those of us who have done several thousand leases, we can assure you. It is never simple.

Why not have a Guide? Especially one you're not paying for but would have the same fiduciary responsibilities as an employee? What do you have to Lose? The answer to that question is in this Leasing Book.

Enjoy! and be prepared to have an Exciting Adventure with a positive outcome. You don't want to be an Example in a Book like this!

Lisa Mininni, Best Selling Author, President, Excellerate Associates

In the book <u>Do You Speak Lease?</u> Lynn Drake has combined her experience in corporate site selection and her experience in commercial brokerage to develop a process that considers both disciplines, which guides the reader to a systemized approach to finding and leasing office, industrial or retail space. This is a must read for anyone who wants to understand the process of how best to find and negotiate a lease for their business.

Do You Speak Lease?

Finding and Negotiating Your Own Commercial Space

By Lynn Drake, MCR

Do You Speak Lease
Finding & Negotiating Your Own Commercial Space

Lynn Drake

Published by:

True North Publishing, LLC
info@truenorthpublishing.us
http://www.truenorthpublishing.us

To order additional copies of Do You Speak Lease, visit: www.doyouspeaklease.com

Copyright 2017 by Lynn Drake

1st Edition

ISBN Print Edition: 978-0-9988495-0-8
ISBN eBook Edition: 978-0-9988495-2-2
ISBN PDF Edition: 978-0-9988495-1-5

DO YOU SPEAK LEASE?

Finding & Negotiating Your Own Commercial Space

INDEX

ABOUT THE AUTHOR

About the Author:

Lynn Drake

Humanitarian, broker, author and entrepreneur, Lynn Drake lives in Troy Michigan. 'Raised in a business home' by her entrepreneur/broker Mom and entrepreneur Dad, she has her Bachelor of Science in Business and a concentration in Accounting, from Oakland University. A Master of Corporate Real Estate (MCR) Certification. Drake is an expert in finding and negotiating office, industrial and retail spaces, with a long-haul experience in almost all areas of commercial real estate. In 2010 she opened her own company called Compass Commercial, a real estate firm, which exclusively represents and strives to protect the interests of the tenants and buyers, as opposed to the landlords.

In 2015 she was honored for her leadership by the SE Girl Scouts of America and was inducted into the Midwest Real Estate Magazine's Hall of Fame.

She has been featured on the Florine Mark's "Remarkable Women" show, and received Crain's Detroit Business Real Estate Excellence Award – 2007.

Do You Speak Lease?

Finding & Negotiating Your Own Commercial Space

By Lynn Drake, MCR

FORWARD:

Starting a new business?

Need office, retail or warehouse space?

Tried calling a realtor and couldn't get your call returned?

Do you prefer a DIY approach?

When you are looking for a residential space, there are laws to protect you from others taking advantage of you. However, in the world of business real estate, it is simply "buyer beware." Each category of real estate has its own terminology, and to make matters more complicated, not all landlords are well-versed in the world of commercial real estate; they just do their own thing. Long story short, the world of commercial real estate is confusing.

Imagine you are driving down the street and you see a beautiful building for lease. You take down the listing agent's phone number to call later. You make the call, but never get a return call. Why is that? I'll explain this phenomenon and so much more...

If you understand the terms and follow my step-by-step directions, you will be armed to meet the challenges of leasing or buying commercial real estate space. In this book, I will define the terms you need to know, discuss the different types of real estate, and provide you with a step-by-step guide to get the job done. Also, included in the book are financial summaries to help you determine the true costs. There is an office space calculator that will help determine how much space is required and an example of a Request for Proposal (RFP) that you can use. You will find short articles that demonstrate the point of each section to help you better understand this crazy world of commercial real estate. Armed with the right tools and a professional approach, you will soon be able to find your business's new home.

Do You Speak Lease?

Finding and Negotiating Your Own Commercial Space

Some of us speak German, Spanish, French or
Mandarin, in addition to English. We think that if
we can speak these other languages, surely, we can
speak real estate. But that's where we're wrong.
See, not everyone can speak commercial real estate.
That's why it's important to understand the fine
print of your lease terms and learn to truly speak
real estate. Without the proper knowledge, you're
risking having lease terms get lost in translation –
and that's something none of us want when we're
putting our office space (and our business) on the
line.

My advice, pay careful attention to how a
commercial or industrial property is listed.

Recently, a client called me, excited to find an
office that you could see from the freeway for rent
at just $1 a square foot. He suggested I drop
everything to check it out. So, I did. As it turned

out, the deal wasn't as attractive as it had seemed, especially when I learned it had been written in California lease language – which meant that the actual rate was $12/square foot. Good, but not extraordinary.

As I looked through the lease, and spoke with the building manager, I found the landlord was unwilling to make any improvements to the space at his expense. Inside the fine print, I found the tenant was responsible for any increase in heating, as well as a maintenance cost to the lobby and halls. Plus, the tenant would be liable for all utilities and janitorial services. The realistic price wasn't $1, or even $12, per square foot. It was $15.50. Not a deal, considering the liabilities.

Becoming well versed in "speaking lease" is the best way to get the best deal. I wish you much success in your search for commercial real estate.

COMMISSIONS

Having spent fifteen years in corporate real estate and having personally completed more than 2,000 transactions, I have had the privilege of working with agents all over the world. Some were great and some were not. When I moved from managing a corporate real estate department in 2000 to the brokerage industry, also known as "the dark side", it really was an eye opener. I was aware from my brief stint working in residential real estate that agents were paid a percentage of the sales price of the house. But, currently, 85% of my time since moving to the "dark side" has been spent on leasing commercial space versus buying and selling it.

There are many types of agents, also referred to as realtors or brokers, which you can learn about more in the "How to Hire a Commercial Agent" chapter. The listing agent receives a percentage of a lease commission and the tenant representative agent also gets a share of the commission. Prospective tenants often think the rent will be cheaper if they don't use an agent. However, less than 5% of the time will this will prove to be true.

Here's why: If the building is listed and the listing agent finds the tenant, either from a rolodex or by calling the number on a lease sign, then he or she will be paid for *both* sides of the transaction. If the building isn't listed with an agent, the commission is often paid to the property manager. In the few instances when there is no listing agent and you are dealing with the owner directly, there will be savings. If you follow my advice and go after two locations at once, you will see in the RFPs that the landlord who most needs to fill his building will be the one to give you the better deal. That may or may not be the "small" landlord that you can work with directly.

Every city and every type of real estate has its own commission structures. I often hear residential agents stating that they get 10% commission for a land deal. Yet, when I've considered this type of sale, no one has ever said the commission is anywhere near this high. Usually a percentage of the rent for the first five years is paid at one rate and then a lesser rate is given for years six through ten. Often nothing for any additional years. This is why you frequently find agents trying to get the lease terms longer than five years, because they make more money by doing it that way.

Please note it is illegal for any agent to pay part of their earned commission to someone who isn't licensed.

When I ran a corporate real estate department, we never signed any leases for more than five years. Business changes and, if you are renting many locations, you may want the ability to relocate or choose a closer location. However, I have a lot of clients who don't like dealing with real estate issues and will ask for a seven or ten-year lease. If this occurs, I also insist on a cancellation option being added to the lease. Usually when this happens, the tenant and landlord agree upfront that at the end of five years the tenant can cancel by paying unamortized improvements and commissions.

Below is an example of what a commission structure might look like:

Square Footage: 1,000
Term: 3 years
Rent: Year 1 $19.00 s/f, Year 2 $19.50 s/f, Year 3 $20.00 s/f

Percentage of Commission paid on a typical transaction: 8% in total with Listing Agent receiving 3% and the Tenant Agent receiving 5%

1,000 x 19.00 = 19,000
1,000 x 19.50 = 19,500
1,000 x 20.00 = 20,000
Total Rent: 58,500
Total Commission   .08
Commission Paid $4,680

Listing Agent Paid: $1,755 and Tenant Agent: $2,925

Note: If there is no tenant agent the listing agent will get either the entire $4,680 or sometimes they will take 7% instead of 8% commission.

THE WORDS

Real Estate Terms Per the Real Estate Dictionary: 7th Edition

Base Year – The year in which a direct expense escalation of rent is based.

Base year is how much the cost of operating a building Common Area Maintenance (CAM) in a year costs the landlord per square foot. If you have a base year lease, you will usually pay any increases of costs over the base year. In 2016 the cost to operate a building is $300,000. At the end of 2017 the cost to operate the building is $309,000. The increase over the base year is $9,000. This cost will be divided by the square feet of the building. 9,000 /50,000 = .18 cents/s.f. If you had a base year of rent of $20.00 s.f. it will increase to $20.18/s.f.

CAM – Stands for "common area maintenance."
So, for example, if we have a 50,000 s.f. building
and the total cost to operate this building in 2016
was $300,000, the cost to operate the building that
year was $6.00/s.f. (300,000/50,000).

Dual Agency – The representation of opposing principals (buyer and seller) at the same time. In brokerage, many states get around this by saying that the agent aids the buyer, but is the agent of the seller only.

In the state of Michigan, the law states that if a brokerage firm has a listing, the rights of that landlord always come before the tenant. In other words, it is the listing agent's duty to get the tenant or the buyer to pay as much money as possible. The tenant or the buyer is under the impression that their interests are being represented when they are not. Note: In residential real estate, agents must identify in

writing who they represent. It is not this way in
commercial real estate.

Evergreening Clause – *A clause found in leases,*
which causes the lease to be automatically renewed
if the tenant doesn't notify the landlord of their
intent not to renew. Typically found in leases for
executive suites. *(See pages 32-33 for more*
information on Executive Suites)

***Furniture & Fixtures* (FFE):** Tenants and
sometimes landlords will build in furniture or a
fixture. A reception desk could be built in and a
sign could be attached to the wall. Determine what
equipment leaves with you when you depart the
space, so there is no question about what is yours
and what is "permanently affixed," thus belonging
to the landlord

Gross Lease – A lease, which obligates the
landlord to pay all or part of the expenses of the

leased property, such as taxes, insurance, maintenance, and utilities.

Hold Over Fee – If a tenant does not renew their lease and stays past their expiration date of the lease, the landlord will charge a percentage above the normal rent. We often see these charges between 125% to 250%, depending on the landlord. For example, if your rent was $5,000 a month, and you had a 200% holdover fee, your rent would be $10,000 for each additional month you stay past the expiration date, without renewing the lease.

Industrial – Used for storage or assemblage of products, this could be computers, cars or toys. This category includes warehouses, production shops, and flex space (i.e. engineering space).

Load Factor – *Rentable space is the amount of rent you pay for in a lease. As a tenant, you will pay for a small percentage of hallways and common areas. Usable square footage is the amount of space within*

the suite you lease. Most office buildings will have
a load factor between 10% and 18%.
Here is an example of how to figure it:
5,800 rentable – 5,000 usable = 800 s.f. To get the
percentage of the load factor, take the 800 s.f./5,800
rentable = 16% load factor. Another way to
calculate this, is if the landlord provides you with
the load factor percentage. In this case, you would
have 5,000 s.f. useable x 1.16% (load factor) =
5,800 rentable.
This is also referred to as, Rentable/Usable Factor.

Net Lease – A lease requiring the tenant to pay, in
addition to a fixed rental rate, the expenses of the
property leased, such as taxes, insurance,
maintenance, etc.

We use the term net/net/net or triple net to define
that the tenant pays all expenses. This can
include a new heating system, plumbing
problems etc. The landlords only take
responsibility for repair or replacement of the

four outer walls and the roof in these types of leases.

Office – A zoning designation allowing businesses to carry on their paperwork rather than manufacturing or sale of inventory to the public on the site. Examples: law firms, insurance firms or accounting firms.

Pass Through – A method of escalation found in modern leases, whereby the tenant directly pays increases in operating expenses of the property.

Personal Guaranty – An agreement to pay a debt from one's personal funds, if the signing company can't meet its rental obligations.

Relocation Clause – *Gives Landlord the right to relocate tenant at any point during the lease.*

Rent – Consideration paid for the occupancy and use of real property. A general term covering any consideration (not only money).

Calculations 1,000 S.F. at $15.00/s.f. =$15,000 annually / 12 = $1,250 /month for the base rent.

Rentable Area – The area for which rent can be charged. Usually a portion of the hallways and bathrooms are included in this number. See load factor for more information.

Retail – Space for lease in malls, strip centers and stand-alone buildings. Services and items are sold at these types of location.

Right of First Refusal – A right, usually given by an owner to a lessee, which gives the lessee first chance to buy the property if the owner decides to sell. The owner must have a legitimate offer which the lessee can match or refuse. If the lessee refuses, the property can then be sold to the offeror.

Useable Area – The amount of space found within a suite, which excludes common areas.

Zoning – The division of a city or county by legislative regulations into areas (zones), specifying the uses allowable for the real property in these areas

Items listed above in italics are defined by the author. The rest of the definitions are from <u>The Real Estate Dictionary</u>.

Talamo J.D., John. *The Real Estate Dictionary.* Seventh Edition. Financial Publishing Company. 2001.

TYPES OF COMMERCIAL SPACE

OFFICE SPACE

The first type of commercial space we'll review is office space. Office buildings can be broken down into three different classes: A, B or C.

If a building is referred to as a Class A, it usually is a building less than 7 years old or it has been updated during that period. The space will usually have many amenities such as a cafeteria, atrium, etc.

A building referred to as Class B may have similar features but it hasn't been updated recently. Or it could be a brand-new building without any amenities, like a large lobby or cafeteria.

Class C buildings are older one or two story buildings. Class C is also used to classify buildings that are old and haven't been well maintained.

To complicate things, office space charges for rentable square footage, not the actual space you are leasing. That is because the public areas make up 10 to 17% of the building. Each tenant is charged a percentage of this common area and it is added to the usable square footage to give the rentable square footage. See the "load factor" under the Words Chapter for an example of how to calculate this percentage.

There is also Flex Space. This is a one-story building with higher ceilings. This type of space can be used for office or storage of materials. This is a hybrid between an office building and a warehouse.

EXECUTIVE SUITE
Many people don't realize there are many alternatives to leasing an entire suite, such as an Executive Suite which are in most major cities. You can lease one small office, mail service,

answering service or a large conference room by the hour. Start small and save your cash for equipment and staff. People often believe the cost of this type of space is way too high. One should realize, that executive suite providers equip your business with a desk, a receptionist, phones and internet. If you add up these costs, the rent isn't really that high as opposed to purchasing each item individually. You can work out of your house and have your mail sent to the executive suite so it looks like you have a big fancy address. If you travel across the country, you'll find that many of the major players lease executive suites nationwide. You can set it up so that you can stop in any of their locations and hang out in their public areas or rent a conference room for a couple of hours. For sales people traveling nationally, this a great benefit that should not be undervalued.

If you would like us to do the footwork for you and find you an executive suite anywhere in the USA send us an email to real.estate.services@compass-commercial.com

In order to start this process for you we will need to know:

- What city you need to be located in.
- When you want to start the lease.
- How long you will need the space.
- How many people will use the space.
- How many desks you need. (Often you can get from 2 to 4 desks in one room)
- What services you would be interested in. (Office, conference room, a mailing address, answering service, use of common areas across the country?)

MEDICAL SPACE

This is office space that has extra parking to accommodate people visiting an office. This category would include Doctors, Dentists, Chiropractors etc. While some office buildings can accommodate a medical use, many won't have the additional parking required by the medical community. Be sure to check with the city to see if your type of medical use is allowed.

Landlords typically expect the tenant to pay for the construction. If you don't have the cash to pay for a medical build out, look for 2nd generation space that doesn't need a lot of modification. Lending for medical and dental is easy to find. Most banks won't even require the doctor to put any money down on a loan for equipment and even for buying a building.

INDUSTRIAL SPACE

Industrial space is where products are manufactured or stored. These buildings have several different features to look at when considering an industrial space. Some features are dock doors versus overhead doors, ceiling height, cranes, and your firm's power requirements. These factors are dependent on what the space is used for. For example, do trucks need to drive into the facility using an overhead door? Or do they need the ability to use a high low truck to move inventory in out of the trailer which requires a dock door? One of the most important factors when looking at an industrial space is making sure the use is compatible with the *zoning ordinance*. See the chapter on zoning for more information.

Industrial space is leased in the same manner as retail. Sometimes landlords pay for improvements and sometimes they don't. It depends on the market, the lease term, the condition, and the proposed use of the space.

STORAGE UNITS

If you are making an item and run out of space in your home, consider leasing a storage unit to store your products. Many times, business owners need an additional 500 to 2,000 s.f. and they go in search of a building to lease. Landlords can't really make money on this small of a transaction. It is extremely hard to find such a small space. The best part of a storage unit is that you aren't taking on any maintenance with the property. You just pay your rent and let the landlord worry about the rest.

RETAIL SPACE

In a retail outlet, the tenant gets what is referred to as a "white box". A "white box" is an empty space; the basics are there, like walls, electrical outlets, bathrooms and cement floor, but nothing more. The tenant then pays for any improvements needed. Be aware, the tenant is usually responsible for repair/replacement of the heating and cooling system (which will be referred to as **HVAC** for the remainder of the book). I find many tenants are surprised to learn this after the fact. These buildings are rented on a net/net/net (also referred to as n/n/n) basis. So, if the rent is $4.50/s.f. and the nets are an additional $2.50/s.f., the cost to the landlord is $7.00/s.f. The tenant must also pay its own utilities and janitorial. Many new businesses don't ask about all the costs involved in leasing space and get a big surprise when the first bill for the triple nets shows up.

IMPORTANT FACTS

In industrial space and retail space it is usually more critical to determine who is paying for everything, from mowing the grass to maintaining and/or replacing the HVAC units. I just went through this with a retail tenant. We had the HVAC unit checked and it was on its last leg. In order to entice the tenant to take the space, the landlord agreed to replace them at their expense. The tenant still needed to carry a maintenance contract on it too. Find out in advance how much this is going to cost per year.

Whenever leasing retail or industrial space have the heating and cooling units checked before you finish your negotiations. Rather than just accepting that you will have to pay for these items, make the following offers instead:

- Agree to hire a reputable firm to manage the units during the term of the lease.

- Ask the landlord to limit the amount of money your firm would have to contribute to repairs bills each year.

- Make sure that if the system is replaced, the landlord handles it and only charges your company amortized appreciation based upon tax laws. This is often the place I find tenants get huge surprises. I came across a dentist once who didn't limit any of these expenses. Not only did he get stuck paying for a new heating system, but he also got stuck paying for a new roof as well.

ZONING CODES & BUILDING PERMITS

Warning: If you are looking at using a building for something other than it was built for, check with the city before proceeding with an offer to lease or buy. If you move ahead with leasing or purchasing space and/or have construction completed without getting permits, the municipality has the right to shut down your business or require that work be torn out and redone according to code.

ZONING CODES

Each municipality has its own zoning codes. These codes are used to define what can and can't be done in a particular part of a city. If you are opening a location in a new city it is useful to call the city and see if they have someone in charge of bringing new business to the city. They will meet with you, find out your needs, and help you work through that community's process. If you are bringing more than ten jobs to their city, there may even be municipal incentives. A 30-minute meeting with city officials could save you hours and hours of time.

For instance, if you want to lease space in a retail facility for an office use, you should check with the municipality first, as they may not allow you to go into a retail building.

Medical space is a tricky one. One would think that if you are going into an office building that you could put a doctor in the same building. Unfortunately, that isn't the case as this type of use has its own zoning code. A few years ago, there was a doctor who leased a beautiful space on Big Beaver in Troy, MI. In the medical business, tenants usually have to do their own improvements. So, this doctor signed a lease and constructed a beautiful space. Not only did he not check the zoning, but he also didn't get a building permit. Two huge mistakes. After the space was built, the city discovered he did not get the correct permits and did not allow him to move into the space.

The reason an office building won't allow a medical practice all has to do with the parking. Medical space requires a higher density of parking due to all the people coming and going from a practice.

Industrial zoning can get even more complicated. In my community, if I wanted to use a space for a purpose that is acceptable in zoning I-3 but the location of the space is in an I-5 district, it means that anything from I-1 to I-5 is allowed in that building so it's okay to put your business there. Double check the zoning ordinance to make sure this is true for the municipality where your space is located.

If you want to build something where it isn't zoned for that use, you will have to talk with the city and possibly apply for a zoning use permit or have a hearing. These changes are usually considered/approved by the Planning Commission.

If you want to appeal the response from the Planning Commission, you can file an appeal and go to the Zoning Boards of Appeals. In cities, you might appeal to the City Council instead.

In Troy, MI, if you need to get the zoning completely changed you will have to go to the Planning Commission, get their approval, and then go to City Council. Of course, every city in America has their own procedures, so start by getting in touch with city officials in order to get some direction.

If you have to apply for a use variance, you should make sure you have at least six extra months set aside to get these approved.

BUILDING PERMITS

Unless you are simply painting and carpeting a space, you will need building permits. Be aware that, in this day and age when everyone is short on time, getting building permits can take a few weeks or up to three months or even longer.

Make sure that when you are planning your site search you determine how long things will take at the city level and add that to your timetable in order to be sure to get work completed when you want.

I usually prefer to have the landlords build out the spaces versus a client doing it themselves. If you have a professional landlord, they will know how to get permits through the city and can usually do a quicker job than you can.

If you take on this job (while working your regular job), you could run into issues and the landlord may have only given you two months of free rent to get permits and build out your space. You could spend months just trying to get your permits approved.

This next example occurred when my chiropractor hired a relative to do the build out of his office space.

Uh Oh! He Did It Himself

In 2015, I had pulled my back and went to visit my chiropractor. When I called to set the appointment, there was an odd message about his office being temporarily relocated. Turns out, the fire suppression failed in his office, going off one night and ruining everything in the suite. He found a friend who allowed him to use his space for just a few months while they got the new space ready for occupancy. (He was on a month-to-month lease in the original space so he just moved out).

One of his clients had a new exercise program so they thought together they could find a great space. When I asked why he hadn't at least called me for advice he didn't really have an explanation other than the new partner wanted to do it on his own. The good news is they found a location with a professional landlord. Going with the theme of doing it themselves, they decided not to pay the landlord for the buildout. They hired their brothers-in-law, who worked primarily in residential repair, assuming it would be much cheaper than going through the landlord. Never mind that the professional landlord's staff knew how to pull permits and get things approved in that city. Would they have made a profit on this construction? Yes, I'm sure they would have made a little money, but, the partners believed the landlord was going to gouge them. Unfortunately, the brothers-in-law were a bit clueless on working in a commercial space. This resulted in having built to a residential specification and being denied for permitting because they were in a flex building. Since it wasn't their primary business, something that should have taken no more than 60 days took 300 days.

If the landlord had done the work, the tenants wouldn't have had to pay rent until the space was delivered with an occupancy permit. Having done several deals in that complex, I also knew that they should have been given money for tenant improvements. Alas, the partners didn't know they could get the landlord to pay for some of this so they paid for the build out themselves. Luckily, the partners had some free rent that helped for the first few months, but afterwards the rent came out of the partners' pockets. Meanwhile, the chiropractor was still paying for space at his other location. It was over a year before the new space was ready. Imagine double rent for at least six months!

Just another classic example of a do-it-yourself project gone wrong!

THE OVERALL LEASE PROCESS DEFINED

If you are renewing your current lease or have found a new location, the process should be the same. We are going to go through each step of this process. You should note that you will be spending at least 20 to 40 hours of your time, if you do this the right way, on a lease less than 1,500 square feet. And up to 200 hours on a larger location. Yes, there are lots of ways to cut corners, but following this process will provide the best end result.

DOUBLE CHECK YOUR CURRENT LEASE

The first thing you should do before starting to look for a new space, if you are in an existing lease, is review your current lease. You need to check and see what date your lease expires. Does the lease require you to notify the landlord if you aren't renewing? *(If you are in an executive suite there is a 99% chance you are required to give a written notice to the landlord to stop the automatic renewal notice or else your term starts all over*

again). If you need to provide a cancellation

notice, go ahead and do that now. You can always

change your mind later. Next, check what the lease

states about holding over. Most leases will charge

you a daily or monthly fee between 125% to 250%

of your rent. If you are looking for new space and

have over 1,500 s.f., you should start your search at

least 6 months in advance. If you have over 5,000

s.f., start your search 9 months to a year out.

Here's an example of what can go wrong if you

forget to check into your lease's expiration date.

Another case of the last minute gotcha:

In the medical world, most doctors must pay for

improvements themselves. A couple of years ago,

one of our agents was at a doctor's office and heard

the receptionist talking to their landlord about

renewing the lease. As soon as she got in front of

the doctor, she asked what the situation was around

his renewal. He told her his lease had expired 90

days ago, and he forgot to discuss a renewal with the landlord. We were asked how we could help and were given a copy of the lease for review.

Three concerns immediately jumped off the page. First, his current rental rate was $5.00/s.f. over market. Second, the landlord had done the construction for this tenant and amortized the construction loan over the term of the lease. The doctor was paying $8.00/s.f. for that loan. Third, the holdover was 200%. This meant the landlord could charge him double the rent and loan amount for every day he didn't renew.

We jumped into action and within 10 days found him several locations in the immediate area that were move-in ready and for significantly less money than he was currently paying. He let the landlord know he wouldn't be staying. After all, the savings with free rent and rate reductions would decrease his lease by over $200,000 over a 5-year period. The landlord wished him well and reminded him that the hold over fees would be about $10,000/month and, since he wouldn't be able to relocate out until the 5th month, he would now owe the landlord $50,000. Or the landlord would allow him to renew at the same terms and conditions of his last lease. If you do the math it makes more sense for the doctor to relocate. However, the doctor didn't have $50,000 sitting around to get out of his lease, so he signed up for another 5-year term. It was sickening to see how a simple missed date cost this doctor hundreds of thousands of dollars.

DEVELOPING YOUR SEARCH CRITERIA

To start, you and your staff should do some thinking about what and how you want to use the space. Are people working in an open environment? Or do they discuss medical or legal issues and need privacy? Do you need conference rooms or small rooms where people can make private phone calls? Do you need to be near your clients or where you can find staff easily? Or do you want to be 10 minutes from your house? Do you need to have public transportation? How about bikes? If you live in Portland Oregon, your staff may prefer to ride a bike to work. Are there places to lock up a bike? Are bikes allowed inside of your space? Or do you work in the Motor City where public transportation is almost nonexistent? Then you may need parking. Would it be helpful to have offices near the airport? What does parking cost? You get the idea; think about anything and everything that can potentially affect your business. Lastly think about the budget. We will get into this later, but be aware that there are a lot of associated costs with a lease that aren't always clear.

SPACE CALCULATOR TO HELP DETERMINE HOW MUCH SPACE YOU NEED

Below is a basic space calculator that lists the different size rooms available. When we work with large clients they usually assign room sizes by title. A president might have a 16 x 16 office. Perhaps a payables clerk sits in a cube. What size cube should that be?

Setting policies based upon title and job responsibilities can save your firm lots of money in the long run. Most offices these days are open environments with more spaces where small teams can work together. Once these sizes are set, they should be put in a document and, whenever a new location needs to be added, all you have to do is fill out the form and you have the required square footage with no debates about positions, etc.

Here are a couple of examples I've seen happen when there were no rules. Many moons ago it was a lot more common for people to drink in the office. If you never experience this, just watch Mad Men. This was a TV series on a 1950's and 60's advertising firm. During my tenure managing corporate real estate departments, I've seen many interesting things, including a built-in bar. I have no idea if the firm's staff put it in or if it was there before they took occupancy. Either way, their square footage was way over stated due to the "bar area". I've even seen individual offices 2 or 3 times larger than a conference room for 12 people. Egos are always a funny thing. I always wonder what employees must say to the president of their company who drops by to see them and finds the employee with a larger, nicer office than the president. There are the people who are super conservative and have everyone squeezed into space so tight that no one is comfortable. One time I came across a man who thought his position was so important and classified that he went out, hired a contractor at his firm's expense, and built himself 12" thick walls so no one could hear what he was saying. This person was at a Fortune 500 company and wasn't even a director.

Using the exhibit below you can calculate how many square feet your firm will need for office space. If you need help with a retail or industrial location, it is a good idea to hire an architect or designer to help you make the best determination.

All of the exhibits in this book are also available at our website in a pdf form so you can print them out and use them. Follow this link: http://www.compass-commercial.com/book-exhibits/

Exhibit A-1: Office Space Calculator (Blank)

Item No#	Space Description	Size	Square Footage	Quantity	Total Square Feet
1	Offices				
2	Executive	15 x 20	300		
3	Large	15 x 15	225		
4	Standard	10 x 15	150		
5	Small	10 x 10	100		

6					
7	**Work Stations**				
8	Large	8 x 8	64		
9	Medium	6 x 6	36		
10	Single Desk	3 x 5	15		
11					
12	**Conference/Training**				
13	Large 15 to 20 Seats	15 x 25	375		
14	Medium 8 to 10 Seats	10 x 25	250		
15	Small 4 to 6	10 x 10	100		
16					
17	**Bathrooms**				
18	In suite, Single Stall Bathroom handicap	8 x 6	48		
19	Regular Bathroom	6 x 6	36		

20					
21	**Other Requirements**				
22	Receptionist no chairs	6 x 6	36		
23	Chairs in Reception Area	3 x 5	15		
24					
25	Coffee Bar	6 x 10	60		
26	Kitchen, no seating	8 x 10	225		
27	Seating/person	3 x 5	15		
28					
29	Large Copy Mail Room	15 x 15	225		
30	Small Copy Mail Room	6 x 10	60		
31					
32	Storage or Phone	4 x 8	32		
33					
34	Large File Cabinets	2 x 3.5	7		

35					
36	Other Requirements				
37					
38					
39	Total S.F. before circulation				
40	Usable Square Footage (Add circulation factor)	Multiply Total S. F. above times either 25% for heavy offices or use 40% with heavy cubicles			
41	Rentable Square Footage	Multiple Usable Square Footage x 1.16 also known as the load factor			

To use the chart above, fill in the quantity of each item. Remember to add current staff and any projected staff that will be hired over the next few years. Rows 36 to 38 provide empty spaces to if you have a special type of room needed that isn't included in this calculator. If you are wondering what size to use for these items just google the description asking for a square footage.

Most office buildings have common area bathrooms. However, some tenants build out individual offices with their own bathrooms. If this is the case you would need to include a bathroom in lines 18 or 19.

Lines 23 and 27 are so you can fill in the number of seats you want in the reception area and kitchen, in addition to lines 22 and 26. If you need a bigger training/conference room than the one provided simply multiple the additional seats needed and multiply that number by 15.

Add up all the numbers from line 1 to 38 and put the total in line 39. Next you will need to have a circulation factor. Multiple the total in line 39 times .25 for a heavy office build or use .40 for a space with lots of cubes. This total will provide you with the total usable square footage in this example. Now you need to add the load factor. I have used an estimate of 16%. Every building and every city is different so you might need to adjust up or down depending on your needs. In the RFP process the landlord should have supplied you with load factor.

Below is an example of a space calculator fully filled out. This prospect needs 4,981 s.f. When doing a site search, you can tell people you need between 4,900 and 5,500 s.f. Remember, we talked about load factors in different buildings which can either positively or negatively affect your end numbers. If you are looking at office space with a lot of columns in it, it will also cause the amount of square footage to increase.

Exhibit A-2 Office Space Calculator completed

Item No#	Space Description	Size	Square Footage	Quantity	Total Square Feet
1	**Offices**				
2	Executive	15 x 20	300	3	900
3	Large	15 x 15	225		
4	Standard	10 x 15	150	3	450

5	Small	10 x 10	100		
6					
7	**Work Stations**				
8	Large	8 x 8	64	15	960
9	Medium	6 x 6	36		
10	Single Desk	3 x 5	15		
11				·	
12	**Conference/Training**				
13	Large 15 to 20 Seats	15 x 25	375	1	375
14	Medium 8 to 10 Seats	10 x 25	250		
15	Small 4 to 6	10 x 10	100		
16					
17	**Bathrooms**				
18	In suite, Single Stall Bathroom handicap				
19	Regular Bathroom				
20					

21	**Other Requirements**				
22	Receptionist no chairs	10 x 10	100	1	100
23	Chairs in Reception Area		25/chair	2	50
24					
25	Coffee Bar	6 x 10	60		
26	Kitchen, no seating		60	1	60
27	Seating/person		25/chair	4	100
28					
29	Large Copy Mail Room	15 x 15	225		
30	Small Copy Mail Room	6 x 10	60		
31					
32	Storage or Phone	10 x 3	30	1	30
33					
34	Large File Cabinets		7	6	42
35					
36	Other Requirements				

37				
38				
39	Total S.F. before circulation	Total rows 1-38	3,067
40	Circulation factor	Multiply row 39 by either 25% or 40% In this instance, we used 40%	1,227
41	Usable Square Footage	Total lines 39 and 40	4,294
42	Rentable Square Footage	Multiple Usable Square Footage x the load factor 1.16 = Rentable Square Footage	4,981

As an extra bonus, our website has a space calculator for you to use that has pictures of each room set up, which makes it easier to determine what size of offices your business needs. Follow the following link to access the online calculator: http://www.compass-commercial.com/space-calculator/

This summary is what you will need to help you determine your company's square footage requirement.

Core-net Global did a study on the average square foot per person and estimated that in 2017 the rate will be down to 151 square feet per person. Back in the 1970's, it wasn't uncommon to see between 250 and 300 s.f. per person.

Here is something for you to ponder when figuring out your company's space needs:

How Many People Can Share a Desk?
In 2013, I sat on a panel led by Knoll with many designers and architects, and we discussed the ratio of people to a desk. In the sales environment, there could be 3 desks set up for 28 people, because they will be in and out of the office all day. Currently at most major companies, the ratio is 2 to 3 per desk. In a sales organization, the ratio can be as high as 20 employees per desk! Lately, the

movement has trended toward an open work environment with several conference rooms and meeting spaces. Last year, we visited Quicken Loans in Detroit, where we saw a completely open concept office with large kitchens, meeting rooms for team work sessions, and smaller rooms for private phone calls. As I look to the future, I see this set up as working well for my own firm. Different size meeting rooms and an open working area make for great working relationships, enabling the creative flow of ideas while also stimulating efficiency.

FINDING THE PROPERTY

Finding potential buildings for lease is much easier now that we have the internet. If you are looking for space by yourself, start your search with LoopNet. LoopNet is a national multi-listing service (MLS) for commercial properties. You can put in your parameters and it will give you sites for lease. Be aware that while this process sounds easy, over 50% of what you find on LoopNet is incorrect. If you are wondering why, let me share a few facts with you. Most listing agents want you to find them so that they potentially have the opportunity to make double the commission. Leaving up bogus listings signs and posting non-existing listings in the MLS gets them more potential customers. The following is a small list of free sites that have commercial properties for lease or sale: https://www.cimls.com; http://www.showcase.com; http://www.loopnet.com. If none of these work for you, search on line how to find sites for lease and you will see more options.

For more unusual requirements, I suggest driving the area you want and looking for signs. You might run across someone who didn't want to list their property and who isn't aware of the online options. I work for the State of Michigan and using the commercial MLS (Costar) in my area doesn't really provide me with enough information. I do the site search the old fashion way - driving the area. As you drive around, take down the address of potential properties and the name and phone number for the listing agent. Please be aware the agent listed on the sign exclusively represents the landlord. Even if this agent acts like he or she is working in your favor, their job is always to get you to pay the most money possible.

Calling the Listing Agent

Now that you have several potential sites, it is time to call or email each agent to get more information. You should be prepared to answer the following questions:

- How many square feet is needed
- When you want to take occupancy
- What lease term you require
- How your business will use the space
- Any unique aspects about your business that could affect your occupancy

Questions to ask the agent:

- Does the landlord have a space available similar to your needs or can they create one?
- What is the cost of rent?
- Is it a gross, modified gross, or net/net/net lease?
- When is the space be available for occupancy?

Below is an example of the form I use when calling available sites. Even as an agent using a MLS that I pay a lot of money for each month, I find at least 50% of the space shown is incorrectly listed.

Under Space Calculators in this book, you figured out how many square feet your group needs. When you call or email the agent, it is a good idea to provide them with the range of square feet needed and the number of rooms. If you can find a space already built out similar to your needs, it will cost you and the landlord less money in the long run by potentially avoiding a build out.

If you are a retailer looking for space, you should ask if there are any companies in the center that are in the same business as you. While a small business may not realize it, you can ask to be the only hair dresser in the complex. This is something we will address further in the RFP. If you leave a message for a person who has the listing and let them know what type of business you are in, it will save you from wasting time, avoiding looking at a retail building where another tenant in the complex has the exclusive use for that category. If you don't get a call back, it may be because the agent knows they can't help you. If you forget to ask this in the initial question, make sure you tell them about the type of retail business you own before setting an appointment for a tour.

Not everyone in retail knows they can ask to be the only hair dresser in the complex. Some landlords won't allow anyone to have an exclusive right anyway. In super retail complexes the building may be broken into 3 or 4 sections and only one type of business can be located per section.

Once you are back in your office, put together a matrix with the information listed below. As you call the agents/landlords it is useful to know who you called and on what date. If you have called someone more than a couple of times and they don't return the call it could be for several reasons:

- The agent may no longer have the listing and the landlord hired someone new to take over.
- The amount of space or type of use you have isn't a good fit for the building.
- If you are a small tenant, the agent might not want to be bothered because they won't make enough money on the transaction. Most landlords aren't interested in having a lot of small tenants because it means more work for them. If your business is

small and you need office space, I suggest looking back at the chapter that covers Executive Suites.

Exhibit B-1: Site Search for Lease/Sale

Address	Brokers Name	Brokers Phone number	Brokers email address	Available for lease?	Rental Rate/s.f.	Tenants Cost? Utilities Janitorial CAM/NNN	Comments
123 Pickle St	Joe Smith	222 222 2222	Jsmith@ abc.com	yes	$20/s.f.	Tenant pays $1.25/s.f. for electrical, janitorial included, base year paid by ll, tenant pays increases	Currently occupied, but tenant is leaving April 30th Left message 3/15

125 Onion	Jerry Noshow	222 243 7654					LM 3/15, 3/16, 3/17, sent email 3/18
124 Mustar d Lane	Sue Clark	222 234 4567	sclark@d ef.com	no			Left message 3/15, space no longer available
256 Catsup	Pat Happy	222 222 9876	Phappy @jkl.co m	yes	$15/s.f.	Tenant responsible for all utilities, janitorial and CAM	Space is vacant and he can show anytime

Remember Cheap Rent May Have Hidden Costs

For everyone that started to believe there really is such a thing as a free lunch and free rent, the game is up. Landlords maybe willing to give a month of free rent, but the incredibly generous deals from 2008 to 2012 are fading as buyer interest picks up. Watch for hidden costs lurking about as landlords seek to recoup costs from the bleak years.

We were hired as a tenant representative for a national firm with a building in Denver. Our needs analysis indicated the client/tenant had about 1,500 square feet more than they should. The local contact swore she needed every square inch, but the home office disagreed. Frankly we couldn't understand why this particular office needed so much space. Something was hidden and our task was to discover where and why.

When we told the landlord, we were representing the tenant, he was unusually angry about our firm stepping in to manage our client's renewal. We explained that all the firm's lease arrangements were handled by a national brokerage firm. He calmed down, but it appeared he was hiding something and so we asked for a request for proposal (RFP) on the lease in question. Once we had the filled out the RFP, the mystery of the phantom space was discovered. The rentable usable factor was 22.5 percent on an old building with no amenities. My client was paying for phantom space – at least 10 percent of its imagined square footage. The landlord knew the jig was up and we moved the tenant to a new location with an honest landlord.

What looked good as a nice round number wasn't a fair price when all factors were included. With the strength of a national organization behind us, we successfully lowered the rate for our client. But the lesson served as a warning for tenants in buildings occupied anywhere in the country: look more closely at this rentable, usable factor (load factor) and see what is actually contained in the number.

HOW TO SET UP A TOUR

Now you should have a list of spaces that are available for lease or purchase. Setting up a tour for commercial real estate is a bit tricky. When we take a client out on tour, we try and set up 4 to 5 appointments, one after the other. The biggest difference in touring residential from commercial real estate is the listing agent will show up for all showings. Here are the steps we take:

1. Using the list of sites for lease in Exhibit B-1, we map the sites to see if there is a way to set up the tour that makes sense. If you are looking at 2 cities, you obviously don't want to cross your way back and forth between each of the cities. You should also look at who has the listings. Let's say Joe Smith has 2 out of 5 listings you want to see. Can you set it up so it isn't disruptive to your tour to see both of his listings one after the other? Usually when I have the same person with multiple listings, we put them last in the tour.

2. When setting appointments, ask the listing agent how long it will take to walk through the property. In buildings with many amenities, the agent will want to show it all off so it could take 30 minutes to see one building. Depending on the building, there could be multiple spaces that meet your needs. You want to make sure you set up enough time to see everything.

3. If possible, get floor plans from the listing agents before the tour. These should be included with the tour package so everyone on your team can take notes.

Now you have your ideal tour order. Using the form below, fill in the order and start setting appointments. If you don't know how long the drive time is, use Google Maps to estimate driving time, taking into account the time of day and drive patterns.

Exhibit C-1: Site Tour

Arrival Time	Street, City	Rental Rate	Agent	Cell Phone Number	Where are you meeting at the property	Comments
1:30	256 Catsup, Anywhere	$15.00 n/n/n	Pat Happy	xxx xxx xxxx	In the lobby of the property	
2:15	123 Pickle St, Somewhere	$20/s.f. plus electric base year 2017	Joe Smith	xxx xxx xxxx	This space has its own entrance in the rear of the building, meet in front of suite 110	
2:45	128 Hamburger Drive, Somewhere	$18.00/s.f. gross	Jolene Smith	xxx xxx xxxx	Meet at suite 150 in the building	
	135 Bun Rd. Somewhere	$17.50 plus utilities	Jolene		Meeting in lobby	

It is critical that you have the cellphone numbers of the agents. On the morning of the tours, call and confirm the times you will be meeting each agent. In the event you are running late, you can call the agents. Sometimes agents run late too. If you show up for an appointment and they aren't there, you can call them to get an estimate of when they will arrive. One late agent and you could get 30 minutes to an hour behind.

As you and your team see each location, take notes. You might even want to create a numerical survey and have everyone rate the buildings while touring. Some items that might be useful to include on a rating scale are:

- exterior
- hallways
- bathrooms
- location,
- parking
- traffic flow
- entrances and exits

- how the grounds are kept
- overall feel of space
- existing tenants
- etc.

It is always interesting to see how each member of a team sees things differently. Unless one is used to looking at several properties at once, the spaces will all blend together, so taking notes and pictures can be helpful later on when you return to the office to discuss.

After the tour, pick 2 to 3 locations to get additional information. Caution, if you only pick one location, it most likely will disappear because landlords often negotiate with several tenants at one time. Another reason to go after more than one location is to create leverage; have the landlords compete for your business. Sometimes we get all the way to the end of negations and the deal falls apart for any number of reasons. So, if you were going after several locations at once, at least you aren't back to square one.

You can set as many tours as you want, but I strongly suggest that somebody drives by the location before setting an actual appointment. Listing agents will always show the best possible picture of the building online or in the MLS. You might show up for a tour and find the city dump is next door; every time the wind blows you and your team will have to hold your noses. Save yourself time and money with a quick drive by.

Managing a corporate real estate department for many years has given me insight into the ways an internal team member might try to throw you off track. If someone doesn't want to drive further to work, they may claim a building is in a dangerous area. You simply can't let this suggestion go unaddressed. If this type of complaint is made, call the police department and find out what the crime statistics are for the area and compare it to the current area you are in.

One time I had a client with an office in California that was literally a block from the LA airport. The head of the office said they had to move because the planes were dropping fuel on the building, causing an odor. I was asked to fly out to investigate. As I'm sure you can imagine, there was no odor. The manager wanted to live closer to her house and this is the complaint that she used to try to manipulate the situation so that she could get her way. Any complaints around health or safety should be reviewed before signing on the dotted line.

PREPARING A REQUEST FOR PROPOSAL (RFP)

So, you and your team have looked at 5 or 6 buildings and are now at the point where you are ready to move forward with 2 locations. However, you see that the top two locations have the same listing agent. I suggest you go after your third choice as well to help create leverage with a different agent.

Most listing agents do not want to fill out RFPs. Without a written response from the agent, negotiated items might be unclear or purposely left vague until the lease is prepared, and then it is too late to go back to a different location because you have run out of time. The agents may assume that you understand that some buildings are gross, some are modified gross, and some are triple net. It is critical that you understand all the costs associated with each type of deal. If they won't fill out the RFP get on the phone with them and ask them to answer each question and you can record it as you go. When you believe all the deal points have been negotiated put all of the terms into a final RFP proposal and make sure everyone is in agreement before a lease is drafted. Unfortunately, I have had to do this myself as well.

A RFP will look like the following sample. Please note highlights indicates that you need to insert what is unique/important to your business.

Exhibit D-1: RFP Filled Out By The Tenant

Item	Tenant's Request	Landlord's Response
Date Requested:	10/1/17	
Requested Response:	10/13/17	
Address:	123 Pickle, Suite 110, Somewhere	
Area:	Approx. 5,000 s.f.	
Occupancy:	May 1, 2018	
Rentable/Usable	What is the rentable/usable factor	
Rent:	Provide a market rent at the same rate throughout the lease	
Free Rent:	Provide free rent	
Tenant Improvement:	Provide a turn key build out based upon the needs analysis which is attached to this rfp	*note use the space calculator from exhibit A-2

Utilities:	Check the items that are the tenants responsibility; also note if the utilities are separately metered or if not, what the annual costs should be	( ) Electric If charged how much annually: $__/s.f. ( ) Gas ( ) Water
Janitorial:	Check is landlord does not provide janitorial	( ) Janitorial Tenant Cost
Additional Expenses:	Check all additional expenses which are tenant's responsibility	Check correct response ( ) Gross lease no additional expenses ( ) Modified Gross tenants, base year is ____ Last year's cam was $____/s.f. Estimate of 20__'s cam charges $__/s.f. ( ) Triple net estimate of 20__ $__ s/f
Who has responsibility for repair/replacing the following items:	Check items which are tenant's responsibility	( ) HVAC ( ) Plumbing ( ) Roof ( ) Landscaping ( ) Parking lot maintenance ( ) Other not listed above
Lease Term:	Provide a 3 year lease	
Access:	Tenant would like access to the premise for installation of wiring and furniture and fixtures one month prior to lease commencement	

Renewal Option:	Tenant request the right to renew the lease for an additional 3 year period at market rate	
Network:	Provide a list of data/phone/internet carrier connectivity in the building	
Parking:	Tenant requests 10 parking spots for its use	

If you would like a pdf of this example follow this link: http://www.compass-commercial.com/book-exhibits/

The following exhibit shows you what the RFP response from a landlord looks like fully filled out.

Exhibit D-2: RFP Filled Out By The Landlord

Item	Tenants Request	Landlord's Response
Date Requested:	10/1/2017	10/14/2017
Response Requested:	10/15/2017	
Address:	123 Pickle, Suite 110, Somewhere	123 Pickle, Suite 110
Area:	Approx. 5,000 s.f.	5,125 rentable S.F.
Occupancy:	5/1/2018	5/1/2018
Rentable/Usable:	What is the rentable/usable factor	16%
Rent:	Provide a market rent at the same rate throughout the lease	$20.00/s.f. with .50 annual increases
Free Rent:	Provide free rent	1 month
Tenant Improvement:	Provide a turn key build out based upon the needs analysis which is at the end of this rfp	Landlord will provide a $30.00/s.f. build out, the balance of any improvements will be due upon lease commencement *

Utilities:	Check the items that are the tenants responsibility; also note if the utilities are separately metered or if not, what the annual costs should be	(x) Electric If charged how much annually: $1.25/s.f. ( ) Gas ( ) Water
Janitorial:	Check if landlord does not provide janitorial	( ) Janitorial Tenant Cost Landlord to provide 5 days per week janitorial

Additional Expenses:	Gross Lease
	Modified Gross Lease with increases over base year, provide base year plus last year's cam and an estimate of this year's cam
	N/N/N
	Check correct response
	( ) Gross lease no additional expenses
	(x) Modified Gross tenants,
	   base year is 2018
	   Last year's cam was $7.60/s.f.
	   Estimate of 2017's cam charges $7.75/s.f.
	( ) Triple net estimate of 20__ $___ s/f	

Who has responsibility for repair/replacing the following items:	Check items which are tenant's responsibility	( ) HVAC ( ) Plumbing ( ) Roof ( ) Landscaping ( ) Parking lot maintenance ( ) other not listed above Landlord is responsible for all maintenance
Lease Term:	Provide a 3 year lease	61 months only Landlord will not do a build out for a three year lease
Access:	Tenant would like access to the premise for installation of wiring and furniture and fixtures one month prior to lease commencement	One month prior
Renewal Option:	Tenant request the right to renew the lease for an additional 3-year period at market rate	Landlord will offer a 5 year renewal option at the prevailing market rate at that time.
Network:	Provide a list of data/phone/internet carrier connectivity in the building	Comcast only

Parking:	Tenant requests 10 parking spots for its use	$150/month for each covered parking spot

*Note in my financial summary example (see exhibit F-1), the build out didn't cover the allowance and the tenant had to pay $5.00/s.f. of the cost. You won't know this until the landlord has priced the entire plan.

What Can You Negotiate Besides Just the Space?

The more you think about what your firm really needs before you start a site search the more successful your search will be. Think about location. Where does your staff live? Does your staff take a bus route or subway to work? If so, it will be critical to identify these items. Some things will have to do with the building itself. For instance, if you need access to the building 24/7, that should be a line item in your request for proposal (RFP) to the landlord. Below are some lists of additional items you may want to add to your request for proposal:

Intended Use: This is particularly important in a retail or industrial building lease

Exclusive Occupancy: Not allowing competitors in your niche to occupy the same building

Building's Zoning: Is your firm's use allowed? (Note: Most landlords won't answer this, they want you to confirm for yourself.)

Cancellation Rights: If you sign a longer-term lease, can you pay to get out of the space on a specified date?

Right of First Refusal: of Adjacent Space: If the space next to yours becomes available, can you lease it for the same rent as you pay in current space?

Subleasing & Assignment Rights: Will you have subleasing and assignment rights? If you don't need your space anymore, what are the subleasing rules?

American with Disabilities Act (ADA) Compliant: Space must be wheelchair accessible. If you have someone apply for a job with your company and you can't hire them because they can't get into the building, you may have a legal issue. Check with your lawyer if you have additional questions on this matter.

Floor Load: If you have heavy equipment, identify what that might be in the RFP.

Expansion Options: If your firm is growing, you may want to expand into the adjacent suite.

Non-Disturbance Agreement: If the landlord has a mortgage on the building, you want protection from the mortgage company so that they won't kick your business out if the landlord defaults on the mortgage

Security: Is security important to you firm?

Signage: This includes on the building, marquee or lobby. What type of signage can you negotiate? Please note: in order to get building signage, you must occupy a good percentage of the building. The cities set the rules on how much signage is allowed on each building. If there is already signage on the building, the landlord may not be able to provide this to you as a tenant.

Parking: Leaving trucks or cars overnight on the property? Make sure you get permission.

Garage: If your firm is located in a city, parking can be crucial. Does the building have parking? If so what is the monthly cost? If the building doesn't have any onsite parking, ask the landlord to identify a location that will provide parking for your team. The cost of parking in a garage can be a big expense for a company, so make sure you identify the monthly costs.

Visitor Parking: Are there people who come to visit your location from time to time and you want to eliminate their search for parking? If so, you can ask that a few spots are designated for parking in front of your space for visitors.

Relocation Clause: Landlords will often request the right to relocate a tenant in the middle of their lease. This is very unproductive for the tenant and should be avoided if possible. If the landlord insists on this clause, make sure the landlord pays for:

- Any improvements made by your firm or the landlord in the original location
- The costs of moving which should include the cost of rewiring the new suite
- The costs of having company literature reprinted, etc.

If the landlord tries to move you to a bigger suite, then the landlord shouldn't be charging you for the extra space. Be aware, this agreement is only good through the end of your lease. Once a new lease term begins, you will be expected to pay for all of the space in your new suite.

Below are some additional examples of things to think about when determining your firm's needs.

Leases and Animals

While many people might consider agents to be animals, the animals I'm referring to here are the four-legged furry types. In 2012, I ran a column asking for the oddest lease clauses that people came across. The most amusing answer I received was for a location where the tenant wanted to bring their dog to work. Per the agent, the landlord agreed that the dog wouldn't wear pink or leather. Nope, I'm not kidding! While funny, the clause didn't cover the true issue: the dog's behavior. What if the dog barked and disturbed other tenants? Where would the dog "do its duty"? What are the consequences if the dog bites? These are the types of issues that should have been covered in the lease.

In the end, here's what it comes down to: if there is something unusual about your business, make sure you address it in the RFP up front in order to avoid running into trouble in the final hours of your lease negotiations.

My Extendable Ears Were Ringing

While eating lunch one day in a Boston Market, I overheard two women talking about their troubles relocating their office. I was desperate to acquire the extendable ears that Harry Potter used in several of his movies, but their voices were loud enough to suffice.

They discussed a long list of questions that popped up after the lease was signed. They fumed about all the uncertainty with new buildings and questioned how this place would accommodate them over time. I was just about to rise up and walk over when they stood to leave. They were in such an emotional flurry, I sat down and concentrated on my newspaper.

As a professional with over two decades experience, it infuriates me to hear about agents who don't supply the potential tenants with financial summaries of the building and floor plans. There are agents that leave more questions unresolved than does a night watching Jeopardy reruns. I worked out my frustration over the delicious cornbread. Had these women consulted with a tenant representative or read this book prior to signing an agreement to lease, they wouldn't have all these unanswered questions. They could step into their new building with eyes wide open.

Who Set the Thermometer?

Your company culture might encourage people to flex their schedules, stay late in the evening, or come in on weekends during crunch periods. Can your building accommodate you? Does it accommodate the hard workers down the hall at your expense? But the even bigger question is, who controls the thermometer?

If a building has an automatic dial down on the furnace at 5 p.m. and dial up at 8 a.m., it might interfere with your operation. Some buildings might charge you a heat/cooling stipend of $50 to $100 an hour when your team is at variance with other tenants. Others might leave the heat or air conditioning unit at the setting 24/7, which spreads the penalty around to all the tenants.

It is good to visit a building on a really cold or really hot day to see how well the HVAC system is distributed around the available space. You might find one sector is freezing while another is roasting. It is easier to make changes or repairs at the start of a lease. If the problem persists, employees could be tempted to bring space heaters to stay warm, which then becomes a fire hazard.

Control of the thermometer is just one item, but it represents a comfort item that is near and dear to employees, the people you most need to keep safe and comfortable.

DEFINING TENANT IMPROVEMENTS TO THE SPACE

There are three ways to negotiate improvements. Before you can begin, you will need to have identified your space needs back in Exhibit A-2.

If you are a firm that needs less than 2,000 s.f., and are less than 5 years old, you are going to want to keep the costs of improvements down. Since the crash of the commercial real estate market in 2008, landlords are a lot less likely to complete improvements for smaller or newer tenants. One issue I see all the time is tenants trying to get the landlords to build in reception desks and half walls to separate their space. Or they pick the most expensive floor/lighting they can find. Then, when the landlord asks for a higher security deposit and a personal guarantee, they are baffled and sometimes think the landlord doesn't want them or their business. That is not the case; the landlord simply wants to make sure they get reimbursed. Newer firms pose a higher risk of bankruptcy than established firms.

My preferred way to ask for improvements is to provide a specific set of improvements. For example, the space needs are as follows: (you fill in the rest). You might request fresh paint, new carpet, or adding/removing a wall. Keeping it simple is more likely to get you a better rate and faster response from the landlord.

If you are looking at undeveloped space (also called "raw" space) you will need to have a designer draw up a plan. It's also possible that the space in consideration is out of date by today's building standards; everything needs to be torn out and built from scratch. In the RFP, provide the landlord the list of rooms you need, requesting that the landlord uses a designer to develop a plan. If you are an office tenant, the landlord will expect to pay for this service. You should ask them to do so in your RFP.

When landlords are building out space, they have something called "Building Standard Materials". This would be for carpet, tile, ceiling tiles, lights, doors etc. When a landlord quotes you a build out, it will be for the building standard materials. For example, carpet tiles are usually more money to install than carpet that comes on a roll. Most landlords will not offer this. For the less expensive buildings you will find the building standards are pretty low. I helped a nonprofit find space just 5 years ago when their previous lease was up. One of the new staff members thought the carpet was so old she refused to take her shoes off and walk around on the carpet. The carpet was only 5 years old; it was simply so cheap it didn't stand up to normal use. The area where I find tenants and landlords most often differ on what is acceptable and what is not, is in flooring and lights. One can go crazy, picking out these items so be careful. If you want above building standard, be aware you will probably have to pay for the upgrades. If you want to make sure you are getting good quality, hire a commercial designer to research and pick out the items for your new space rather than leave it to the landlord's discretion.

If you are in industrial or retail space, however, it is hard to say if the landlord will pay for these upgrades or not. There are many factors the landlord will consider before making this decision. Traditionally, these types of landlords expect the tenant to pay for their own improvements. Sometimes, the landlord will provide tenant improvement dollars, but typically they will increase the rent to pay for these costs. Across the Unites States, different regions do things slightly differently, so you need to find out what is typical in your specific market.

Often the appointments for a design will take place at the proposed location. Make sure you bring the sizes of your furniture to the meeting so you know everything will fit. Expect to request a couple of changes to the plan once the initial plan is complete.

Sometimes landlords will pay for up to two changes to the plan, leaving you responsible for paying for any additional changes.

Once the plan is complete and approved, the plan will be sent out to the landlord's staff or third party construction companies to get a bid. Here are where the two different schools of thought come in.

Some landlords want to give you a tenant improvement allowance. If you are renting 1,000 s.f., for example, they will give you a $15.00/s.f. allowance which equals $15,000. If you agree to this amount and the cost exceeds $15,000, you will have to come up with the cash. Sometimes you can ask the landlord to amortize the extra cost over the term of the lease. If the cost comes in at $20/s.f. then there is a $5,000 difference owed. An interest rate is set and the term of the loan equals the lease term. This monthly cost is computed the same way one would figure out a car loan.

Another way to deal with this overage is to "value engineer" the plan. What this means is to look for places to save money. Perhaps your team wanted hardwood floors and side lights in each office. Could you take out the side lights? Could you use a vinyl that looks like wood but costs way less? The designer can help you make these decisions.

The way I prefer to work is to get the plan down to a turnkey arrangement. This means the landlord agrees to complete the construction with no increases. If you were able to cut the costs of the build to $15.00/s.f., the landlord takes full responsibility for any overages which they missed. When you are on tight budget, this way works best. Since it is the landlord's building, if they missed something in the bid process, it becomes their responsibility. Needless to say, this can get very sticky, which is why it's so important to plan and to check (and double check) your agreements.

REVIEWING AND ANALYZING THE FINANCIALS OF EACH SPACE

Unfortunately, the one thing you can count on with commercial real estate is that very little of it is consistent. In the following examples, I will show you how most landlords and agents cost out real estate. Beware and make sure you get all the costs from the landlord to complete a financial summary.

Follow along on **Exhibit E** will help demonstrate the points we will go over.

Exhibit E-1: Financial Analysis Deal Points for an Office Transaction:

Address	123 Pickle	Assumptions
Type of Space	Office	
Lease Start Date	1/1/17	
Square Footage	5,000	

Rent/S.F. Year 1	$20.00	
Rent/S.F. Year 2	$20.50	
Ren/S.F. Year 3	$21.00	
Rent/S.F. Year 4	$21.50	
Rent/S.F. Year 5	$22.00	
Free Rent	1 month	
Base year	2018	
Base year amount/S.F.	$7.75	Assume 3% annual increase
Electric (assume 3% annual increase)	$1.25	Assume 3% annual increase

Gas	included	Assume 3% annual increase
Water	included	Assume 3% annual increase
Parking/Spot/Month	$150/spot/month	Assume 3% annual increase

Parking Spots	30	
Tenant Improvement/S.F.	$35.00	
Amount Paid for by Landlord	$30.00	
Tenant Improvement Balance	$5.00	Due upon lease execution

Cash Flow for 123 Pickle

Description	Year 1	Year 2	Year 3	Year 4	Year 5	Total
Rent:	100,000	102,500	105,000	107,500	110,000	525,000
Free Rent:	-8,333					-8,333
Increase over Base year		1,163	1,197	1,233	1,270	4,863
Electrical	6,250	6,438	6,631	6,830	7,034	33,182
Parking	54,000	55,620	57,289	59,007	60,777	286,693

Tenant Improvement	25,000					25,000
Total Costs	176,917	165,720	170,117	174,570	179,082	866,406

$100,000. Each year the rent goes up .50/s.f.

Rent Calculation

In this instance, the tenant negotiated one month of free rent.

5,000 s.f. x $20.00/s.f.= 100,000 /12 months = $8,333

In 2016, an investor called me to get a market rate for his new building in Ferndale, MI. When I quoted him a rate of $16.00/s.f. per year he was ecstatic. I remember thinking, "Now that is an odd response," and asked what state he was calling from. As I suspected, he was from California. The rent in California terms was $1.33 s.f./month. He was assuming that I meant $16.00 s.f./month x 12 months = $192/year. It was opposite. I heard his voice drop down and the excitement gone. This is similar to the example given in the first chapter of the book, where a tenant was quoted a $1/s.f. for rent in California language. But in that case, the landlord in that instance was unethical, not wanting the tenant to understand the true costs.

Base Rental Calculation for Californians

$16.00 s.f./year / 12 months = $1.33/month

For the increases over the base year, in the example provided below, it assumes the first month of the lease is the first day of the year, so you wouldn't expect an increase for an entire 12 months. However, if the lease began July 1, 2017, the common area increase over the base rent would actually start 1/1/18 and, therefore, would have 6 months of increased expenses over the base year charged to the tenant in the first year of the lease. This is important because base years follow the calendar. For instance, in our example we had assumed the increase in the base year (which is also referred to as operating expenses) would increase by 3% annually. The better way to estimate this cost is to ask the landlord to provide you a three-year history of operating costs and then figure out how much each year increases, taking an average of the three years. Many landlords do not like to share these amounts unless they are trending downward, so you have to use an alternative amount. If the landlord won't provide this to you, beware.

In this example, where the lease starts 1/1/17, the base year increases won't start until 1/1/18 so there is nothing to calculate in the first year

Tenant Improvement Calculations

The goal with tenant improvements is to have the landlord pay for as many of the improvements as necessary. If you ask the landlord to add a kitchen with lots of upgrades, the tenant improvement allowance may become too much for the landlord, and the tenant will have to pay for part of the bill.

In our example, we assumed the landlord would pay for $30.00/s.f. and the cost was $35.00/s.f. The extra $5.00/s.f. could be paid up front or the landlord might give you a loan similar to a car loan, letting you pay for the loan at a set interest rate over the term of the lease.

Here's a simple equation for this:
Total tenant improvement per square foot minus the amount landlord is paying towards the improvements, equals the amount due.

$35.00/s.f. -$30.00/s.f. from the landlord =$5.00/s.f. owed

If the money for construction is due upon lease execution, the tenant will have to provide a check for the difference.

$5.00/s.f. tenants share of construction times 5,000 s.f. of space = $25,000

Increase Over Base Year in Year 2

5,000 s.f. x $7.75 base year cam x .03%= $1,163

1,163 / 12 months and the rent will go up by $96.92/month in year 2.

Utilities Calculation

The square footage is multiplied by the cost/s.f. In our example the tenant is only paying directly for the electrical costs.

5,000 s.f. x $1.25/s.f. = $6,250/year

6,250/12 months = $520.83/month

Parking Calculations

Parking costs can get complicated. Depending on the location, you may have some parking spots that are more expensive than another. To keep this narrative simple, I've assumed everyone has the same rental rate per parking spot. Parking spaces are usually rented out on a monthly basis. You would need to multiply the number of spaces by the cost per space by 12 months.

30 spots x $150/spot x 12 months = $54,000

$54,000 / 12 months =$4,500/month

Retail/Industrial Financial Summary

Since both of these types of real estate are usually leased on a net/net/net basis, the costs are going to be different than for the typical office lease. Below you will find a blank copy of what is required and how to calculate these costs.

Exhibit F-1 Blank Retail/Industrial Financial Summary

Retail or Industrial Transaction	Description	Explanation
Address		
Type of Space		

Lease Start Date		
Square Footage		
Rent/S.F. Year 1		
Rent/S.F. Year 2		
Ren/S.F. Year 3		
Rent/S.F. Year 4		
Rent/S.F. Year 5		
Free Rent		
Base year		
Operating Expenses AKA N/N/N		
Electric		
Gas		
Water		
Janitorial		
Parking/Spot/Month		

Number of HVAC Units		
Tenant Improvement Cost/S.F.		
Landlord Improvements Allowance?		
Tenant Improvement Balance		

Cash Flow For Retail or Industrial (Blank)

Description	Year 1	Year 2	Year 3	Year 4	Year 5	Total
Rent:						
Free Rent:						
Operating Expenses *or N/N/N						

Undefined Cost						
Electrical						
Gas						
Water						
Heating & Cooling Maintenance						
Parking Fee for Semi's						
Janitorial						
Build out Cost for Tenant						
Total Cost/ Year						

(AKA Operating Expenses), Taxes, and Insurance. There are many ways to break these costs down, but make sure the landlord has provided you with the correct information.

Exhibit F-2 Completed Deal Points and Cash Flow for Retail or Industrial

Retail or Industrial Transaction	Description	Explanation
Address	130 Hot Dog	
Type of Space	Retail	
Lease Start Date	1/1/2017	
Square Footage	4,900	
Rent/S.F. Year 1	$12.00	
Rent/S.F. Year 2	$12.00	
Ren/S.F. Year 3	$13.00	
Rent/S.F. Year 4	$13.00	
Rent/S.F. Year 5	$13.50	
Free Rent	0	
Base year	0	Because this lease is a N/N/N, there is no base year.

Operating Expenses AKA N/N/N	$6.25	(assume 3% annual increase)
Electric	$1.25	(assume 3% annual increase)
Gas	$0.75	(assume 3% annual increase)
Water	$0.50	(assume 3% annual increase)
Janitorial	$1.50	(assume 3% annual increase)
Parking/Spot/Month	0.00	(assume 3% annual increase)
Parking Spots	0.00	
HVAC Maintenance Contract/Unit	$500.00	(assume 3% annual increase)
Number of HVAC Units	2	
Tenant Improvement/S.F.	$37.00	
Amount Paid for by Landlord	0.00	
Tenant Improvement Balance	$37.00	

Description	Year 1	Year 2	Year 3	Year 4	Year 5	Total
Rent:	58,800	58,800	63,700	63,700	66,150	311,150
Free Rent:						
Operating Expenses or N/N/N	30,625	31,544	32,490	33,465	34,469	162,592
Electrical	6,125	6,309	6,498	6,693	6,894	32,518
Gas	3,675	3,785	3,899	4,016	4,136	19,511
Water	2,450	2,524	2,599	2,678	2,758	13,009
Janitorial	7,350	7,571	7,798	8,032	8,272	39,022
HVAC Maintenance Contract	1,000	1,030	1,061	1,093	1,126	5,309
Parking	0	0	0	0	0	0
Tenant Improvement	*181,300					181,300
Total Annual Costs	291,325	111,563	118,045	119,676	123,805	764,414
Monthly Costs	9,168	9,297	9,837	9,973	10,371	

*$181,300 is due at lease execution in this scenario.

There are some differences in the how the costs are charged between office and retail/industrial. The biggest difference is the operating costs are generally included in the office lease, hence the higher rent/s.f. and on lease terms of 5 years the landlord will kick in some tenant improvement dollars. However, in the medical business the landlords generally don't pay for improvements.

In a retail or industrial scenario, the tenant is paying the net charges, also known as the operating expenses. These costs should include insurance on the entire building, taxes, landscaping, snow removal and any costs to maintain the building. Generally, in a retail or industrial lease, the tenant is also responsible for repair and/or replacement of the heating and cooling unit, plumbing and the roof. In this instance, the tenant agrees to pay for a maintenance contract on the HVAC unit. In exchange for this, the landlord agrees to set a cap on additional expenses for this cost. Without this being spelled out in the lease, a tenant could get stuck paying for an entirely new system. Anything that breaks outside of the four walls could be the tenant's responsibility. It is critical that you ask a lot of questions about how these expenses are charged and make sure the responsibilities are clearly spelled out in the contract. Any decisions on what is included and what isn't must be in the lease before you sign it. Not understanding the lease upon signing means you are subject to whatever it states.

In our example the difference between the two models is how the operating expenses are charged - utilities and janitorial become the tenant's responsibility along with any construction. While the two spaces are of similar size, the retail space is less expensive in the end. The office space had to pay $150/parking spot/month, making their cost higher than the retail space, which was not charged for parking. It is important to run these numbers to make sure you can see the real difference in total costs.

If you have two different terms, look at the shortest term and compare the rest of the spaces for the same number of months.

The following are some things to keep in mind:

• In a retail transaction, the landlord should take the space back to a white box. This means there is no dry wall or finished ceilings. When starting from this point one must hire a designer to complete a plan. The designer can also create a plan that calls out all the finishes. Someone needs to apply for permits and build out the space. These additional expenses need to be taken into consideration. A good designer/architect can save you time and money by calling out all the finishes so the space is built to specs. This is also helps when you have contractors estimating the costs. You will get an apple to apples comparison.

• In a retail transaction, you should figure out how long construction and permits are going to take so you can negotiate the space for free during this period. This should be a part of your initial RFP. Asking for this near the end of the negotiations won't go over well with the landlord. The landlord has made their rental offers based upon your request. If you throw in a totally new request the original RFP may no longer apply.

- If you are going to be located in a shared industrial building, your RFP should include how shared areas will be managed. If you are going to share a dock door, for example, make sure you are given access to this door from the interior space so you can move your inventory accordingly. Sometimes a company will lease industrial space without an office. Make sure there will be access to at least one bathroom. If you need office space and there isn't any left in the building, you might look at renting a mobile office as an option. Be aware you will need permits and a way to hook up to the electrical as well.

Below is yet another way to think about these expenses.

Do You Need Your Office Cleaned?

Janitorial is one of the items where we see a wide gap in what landlords provide. Some provide it and some don't. Some will come in once a week and some will come in every day. I was working with a nonprofit and got them cleaning services with their lease. They thought I was brilliant. All I did was ask. This saved them about $1.00/s.f./year. One landlord in the Detroit area started putting in their full-service leases that they won't include the cleaning during the free rent period. I'm thinking surely this is a mistake. Nope, the landlord figured people weren't reading the RFPs or the leases (which is sadly often the case), and was getting away with it.

When you are comparing locations, make sure you compare apples to apples, because bananas and apples only mix well in a fruit salad.

What is With the Electrical Costs?

Across the country, we see different rates for electricity charged by owners, based on their various climates. An electrical rate in Troy, Michigan is going to be far different than one charged in Phoenix, Arizona. But, two buildings in Troy, MI could still have very different electrical costs based on how the landlord handles it. The point of this story is to make people aware that even in the same area, landlords can be charging far more than their neighbors. Why? Usually, it is a cost center for the landlord.

We were working on a project here in Troy on Kirts Blvd. Two buildings, almost identical. One was charging $1.80/s.f. for electric and the second one was charging $1.25/s.f. I was positive that the first agent made a mistake, given what adds up to be a big difference in cost. The rental rate was lower at the location with the higher electrical, which still resulted in an overall higher cost per square foot. Most people would have never have asked and missed the higher costs.

Who Said I Should Pay for a New Heating and Cooling Unit?

In the spring of 2015, I got a 22% increase in my common area maintenance (CAM) pass-through expense. CAM charges are billed pro rata to me and other tenants, based on our percentage of total property square footage and to cover the cost of common area upkeep.

When I sent an email to the property management office asking for clarification, I was told they would get back with me. Several emails later, they finally sent me the itemized breakdown of expenses. As I scanned through the breakdown, I noticed a big spike in the maintenance and repair section of the expenses.

I called the office and asked if they had installed a new heating and cooling system. Their response? "Why yes, we have. Why did you ask?"

I pointed out to the woman I spoke with that she needed to read the paragraph in the lease that defined what was an acceptable pass-through expense. It specified that a new HVAC system was a capital expense and that capital expense charges that could be billed to tenants via CAM were limited to the depreciation amount for the useful life of the asset. Before I signed the lease, I realized that 100% of capital improvements could be charged directly to the tenant. I had requested a change to the lease document which stated that capital expenditures needed to be amortized over the useful life of the capital expenses. In this case, the capital expense was the HVAC unit.

By the time we completed the review of depreciation allocation, my CAM charges increased by only 3%.

Counter Offers

Now we have our two RFPs back and have completed the financial summaries. If one landlord provides me a response to one RFP prior to the other ones, I prefer to wait to hear back from the others before responding if possible. It makes it easier to understand the total picture and keeps all the landlords on the same timeline.

If you counter with a rental rate number that is substantially different than what the landlord proposed, the landlord won't respond back to you because they won't take you seriously. Often perspective tenants see a building that has been vacant for a long period of time and can't understand why the landlord wouldn't take the offer. Most landlords have mortgages on their buildings. In the world of commercial lending, the mortgages may be amortized for 15, 20, or even 30 years, but the number of years a bank will provide funding is usually between 5 and 7 years. The banks look at the cash flow of a building to determine its value. If a landlord starts giving the space away for less than market value they won't be able to get a mortgage on the space when their time is up. That is exactly what happened between 2008 and 2013; landlords who had owned their buildings for years and years couldn't get them refinanced and a lot of the buildings went back to the bank. When landlords get behind in their mortgage, the banks will require to approve all rental rates.

Then there are the landlords who have owned the property forever. Some of them might be buying up pieces of land so in the future they can build a specific type of property. While they do so, they only take short term leases so the property will be empty when they are ready. There are the much older landlords out there that bought their properties 20, 30 or even 40 years ago, and it isn't worth it to them to take a tenant on who is looking for a bargain or who only wants a small portion of a big building. It isn't as cost effective for a landlord to have ten tenants when they can have just one or two.

Before countering look at the responses from the different landlords. Do you see any trends? If they all responded with the same rental rate, you have most likely found the market rate. When negotiating if you want to reduce your rent by .50/s.f. then ask for a reduction of $1.00. Most likely the landlord will counter back at .50/s.f., reduction.

Another tactic I use is to share the RFPs with the
different landlords. So, let's say we get an RFP
back on Pickle St and Bun St. If Bun St. is an entire
$1.00/s.f. more per square foot (assuming you have
taken into account the total cost for each location), I
would call the agent/landlord and ask them why
their building is so much more money than other
options in the area. There may be a reason for the
difference, like amenities that makes sense, or it
may be that the owner has a big ego, believing his
building is worth more. It is helpful to make the
counter back to each of the buildings at the same
time. Now the deals are in sync.

It almost always happens and yet it always surprises
me when I'm just about to make a final decision on
a space and one landlord suddenly gets aggressive
and decides make a final "offer". Sometimes near
the end of a negotiation the responses in writing
stops and becomes verbal. Once you believe you
have come to a conclusion on both sides, send the
agent/landlord back the RFP with the final terms.

That way, if something got lost in the translation, you aren't kicking yourself in the end when it is too late to go back to the other landlord and take their deal.

THE LEASE

You are getting close now, so make sure you keep on course and complete the final steps. Let the landlord know you would like a copy of the lease. When it arrives, pull out the final RFP and make sure that every agreed upon term is in the lease. Double check the rental amounts and make sure that the math all adds up. If the rent is $24.00/s.f. for 5,000 s.f. in year one and the rent should be $10,000/month in the first year. Do this for each year and if there is total money owed, make sure that number totals up as well. Below is an example of how to calculate this rent:

24.00 x 5,000 = 120,000 /year
120,000 /12 months = 10,000/month.

Although I'm not an attorney, I have personally
read over 2,000 leases. There are common mistakes
I see in them over and over again. The following is
a checklist with the location of each item placed
under paragraph. It is very helpful to make sure
nothing is missed:

Exhibit G-1: Items To Review In The Lease

Description	Yes	No	Paragraph	Notes
Your Entity's Name is Correct				
Address of Property is correct?				
Landlords name and address is listed				
The lease term is correct				
The rents are correct				
Base Year Listed				

Utilities Defined				
Janitorial Defined				
Amount of Security Deposit				
Insurance Requirements				
Improvements outlined				
Floor plan (attached and correct)				
Exhibit A (included and correct)				
Exhibit B (included and correct)				
Other important items to review				

READ IT!!!!

I cannot stress enough the importance of reading the entire lease. Mistakes are made when people skim and skip, and you could end up paying for something that wasn't a part of the initial deal. Tenants leasing retail and industrial space need to determine if they have any responsibility for maintaining and or replacing capital expenditures. While these items should have been addressed in the RFP, they often get forgotten in all the details. I know it is boring because I read every single lease that comes across my desk, but the surprises you find here could make or break your business. I often find odd clauses thrown into the building rules.

Hire an Attorney Who Specializes in Commercial Real Estate

Law firms are similar to commercial agents. They have many specialties. Often, we find small businesses use the same attorney to negotiate all of their legal needs. An attorney who doesn't specialize in real estate will miss half the items I addressed in this book, and even I can't possibly cover every conceivable thing to watch out for. I will give you an example, one that I will never forget and hope that you will never forget either.

Many years ago, I was working with an attorney who specialized in real estate transactions, or so they told me. I was reviewing a lease she did for someone else and found horrible errors. These mistakes cost my client thousands of dollars. Then shortly afterwards, I was helping this same attorney find an office. When we were done looking at space, they questioned me on every single cost. They acted as if I didn't know the difference between a n/n/n lease and a modified gross lease. Later, I learned they had signed an office lease, not understanding that it was a net/net/net lease and ended up getting stuck paying an extra $5.00/s.f. Just because they didn't know what they were doing, didn't mean that I didn't know how things were done. Ask your attorney just a few questions to see where they stand on real estate. If your attorney hasn't completed at least thirty lease reviews, ask for a referral to an attorney that specializes in real estate.

Lease Execution

When the lease is ready for execution, the landlord will expect a copy of certificate of insurance, 1st month's rent, any tenant improvement dollars owed, and the security deposit. If you had negotiated free rent up front, the landlord will still insist on that first month's rent at the time of signing.

In the lease, fill in any missing dates, initial every page, sign the signature page (usually near the back of the agreement), and if a notary is required go to your bank to get that completed. Ask your landlord how many signed copies are required. If the landlord will accept a scanned copy even better. When you send a scanned copy of the signed agreement scan and send all the pages. The landlord should return the signed document within a week. If for some reason it isn't back by then, follow up. You never know what can change after you have signed a document. You don't want to get surprised when the landlord won't move forward a month later. Until the documents are signed by both sides there isn't a binding agreement, unless both parties signed off on a binding letter of intent. Usually we see a letter of intent used for the sale/purchase of a building or a retail transaction.

Before you do anything else, enter any important dates for your new space in your calendar. If you negotiated a renewal option, record the date the notice must be given plus give yourself a notice 90 days ahead so your team can assess if you want to stay. If you have an early lease cancellation option, record the due date and a date 90 days ahead of time. Capture the lease expiration date and add that to the calendar, plus a date 6 months to 9 months prior to the expiration date. Without these critical dates in your calendar you could miss a very important date that could cost you a lot of money.

A tenant whom I met half way through their landlord negotiations called me for advice when things weren't moving along as they should. The lease had been signed and the tenant was ready to move in, but the landlord invoked their right to relocate them into another space.

The Relocation Clause

Each year, I'm amazed at the new things I see happening with tenants. One of the largest buildings near us in Southfield, MI has taken the relocation clause to new heights. A perspective tenant worked diligently with their soon-to-be new landlord to get their proposed office space just right. No sooner was the lease signed when they were notified that the landlord was moving them into temporary space because another tenant had exercised their right to take the space after the lease was signed.

This should have never happened! Rights of first refusals should always be determined **before** a new lease is signed. This is standard and common procedure with most landlords.

As the horror story above unfolded, I found out that their "agent" represented the building as well. This is, in my opinion, very bad business – for the agent to play both sides. The agent in question had always had their landlord's best intentions at heart, not the tenants. When it came time negotiate the deal, he rounded up the tenant and simply turned them over to the property manager of the building. The tenant had no choice but to move into the temporary space and to begin space planning all over again, starting from scratch after all the work they'd put into their original plan!

This didn't work in anyone's favor financially. The landlord had to pay to move them twice and the cost to the tenant's business with all the moving was simply staggering. Here's hoping you never find yourself in this situation! But, just in case, always ensure that you're working with an agent who works for only YOU, not you AND the landlord!

CONSTRUCTION & TIMING

Once the lease is executed, the landlord will begin construction. If you are having something other than just paint and carpet added, you need to know how long it is going to take the landlord to deliver the space. If walls are being moved, building permits need to be pulled. Every municipality has different timelines. Expect, at a minimum, a month to pull a permit. The landlord should be able provide an estimate of timing with the city and construction. If the buildout is more than just a few walls, construction could take up to 6 months. Paint and carpet can usually be completed in 2 to 4 weeks. One factor that can really cause an issue with a timeline is carpet. When picking carpet, have the landlord make sure your carpet is delivery-ready. If the landlord can't check in advance on availability, and you are short on time, pick out one or two alternative options. The goal is to get your team into your new space as quickly as possible.

If you negotiated a set dollar amount for Tenant Improvements and the landlord is doing the work, I strongly advise you hire a project manager. Their job is to make sure the landlord properly bids out the work and completes the work as shown in the design. This type of service is usually charged based upon the square footage. If you need a recommendation on having someone to do this for you, please let us know and we can happily make a recommendation.

Another critical piece to a move is getting your phones and internet moved and installed in a timely manner. While working through the RFP process you should have identified which companies have service in the building you are moving to. Depending on your needs, and who the carriers are, relocating the space can take from 30 days to 90 days. If your firm is large with special needs the timing could be longer. You don't want to get stuck paying for rent if you can't move in without internet. The landlord is not going to be a nice guy and let you do this either. This is a critical piece that can cause a lot of issues.

If you are moving near the end of the month, get your movers lined up way in advance. Check your lease's rules to determine if there are certain hours in which you can't move in. If you need an elevator, the landlord will be even more picky about the times. If the listing agent verbally tells you can move in whenever you want do not believe him. He doesn't manage the building and shouldn't be making such promise. I've seen many tenants rely on what the landlord representative says and then end up having an issue.

Keep in mind that if you are ordering new furniture, it can take up to 3 months to get it built and delivered.

There are endless details to be dealt with during a move, but the telecom and internet are the two that most often cause an issue for the tenant.

TAKING OCCUPANCY

The landlord should keep you abreast of when the space is ready. Usually the landlord will allow your contractors to work side by side with the construction people for installation cabling and phones without paying for rent. Sometimes you can even move in new furniture if it isn't in the way of the contractors.

Some landlords in my market never deliver the space on time. So the lease provides for a commencement date amendment. This is important because the expiration date of the lease will move accordingly. Let's say you are supposed to take possession on 3/15/17. The city didn't give the landlord an occupancy permit because their staff was out on vacation. You can't get into the space until 4/1/17. If you had signed up for a 3 year lease the original expiration date would have been 3/14/20, but now it will expire 3/31/20. If this happens, go back to your calendar dates and make sure you have the right dates recorded.

Double check with everyone, who is supposed to show up on the move date in advance. Make sure you have the all-clear signal from the landlord. If you are moving from another building all your file cabinets and drawers should be emptied and put into boxes.

Take note of anything that isn't completed when you move in. Ask the landlord to do a walk thru the space with you and make a punch list of unfinished items. If the landlord can't be there for the walk through, make a list of any issues and send to them ASAP.

LEASING SUMMARY

Leasing space can either be complicated or it can be easy. The more you understand the process, the smoother it will go.

The third section of the book has examples of things that I have seen over the years. Some of it goes back to when I managed real estate transaction for my employers, and the rest of it is from my years working as an agent/broker. Many people don't realize how complicated, or time consuming, it can be to do a transaction correctly. Can you do all of this in four weeks? Yes, you can, but I strongly recommend that you don't do it that way, because it is too easy to make a mistake.

RENEWALS: WHAT DO YOU REALLY NEED TO KNOW

Experience has taught me that most people think renewing their lease is simply a matter of getting a rental rate from the landlord and then signing off on a new amendment. One could certainly do that, and your landlord hopes you do. But, hopefully, upon reading my advice, you had the renewal date in your calendar and received a notice from yourself 3 to 4 months ahead of time. Having time to do some research can save you so much money and stress down the road.

Some Things You Should Consider:

• **What is the current rental rate for space in your area?** Most office landlords want a .50/s.f. increase. Unless your firm is located on one of the coasts (where prices go up quicker than the rest of the country), you may be overpaying for your rent by the time the initial lease term expires.

Look at what rental rates are in your area by reviewing rental rates in loopnet.com. When reviewing these rates, you want to remember this is the asking rate, not the rate they actually agreed upon when signing a lease. Additionally, talk to new tenants in your building and ask them about the rates they are paying for signing a new lease, but also how much of a build out the landlord provided. Did they get free rent during the build out? Make sure to ask if they got a modified gross lease or a net/net/net lease. Most landlords won't provide as many incentives to keep a tenant as they will to get a new tenant, but they should be able to offer some type of incentive, especially if you know what to ask for.

The longer the lease, the more incentives you should get for renewals. If you are signing a new seven-year lease, make sure the space gets new carpet and paint. If you are signing a one year lease don't expect the landlord to really do much of anything. A landlord can't take a one year lease to the bank to refinance his mortgage.

During my years in corporate real estate, the number one item missed in a renewal was resetting the base year in a new lease. If you have been in the same lease for 5 or 7 years, your firm could easily be paying between a $1.00 and $2.00/square foot more in pass throughs which should be reset to the current year. Most landlords are not going to bring this to your attention. Remember, this is how they make money.

If your firm leases space in a city and you pay for parking, you need to understand these rental rates as well. I was working with a client who had only 10 parking spaces. Their location was under high demand, so when the lease expired the landlord raised the parking cost from nothing to $250/month per spot. This was a non-profit and this cost doubled their rent, forcing us to relocate them.

- **Is the space still meeting your firm's needs?**
Go back to the chapter on the Space Calculator
that has the needs analysis and fill out the forms
again. If your space is too small or too big, then
you can ask the landlord to move you into a newer
location within the building.

- **Are there some worrisome things going on with
your space?** For instance, is your space being
cleaned? Is the property being properly managed?
Did a new tenant come in and take up all the
parking? These items need to be addressed now
before you sign off on a new lease.

The way I drive my client's rental rates down the
most is going to the market before the renewal
notices are due and getting requests for proposals
from competing properties. However, if you are in
a class A building and get a proposal from a class C
building don't expect the landlord to pay to close of
attention. Approaching your landlord about a
renewal is a totally different conversation than

asking the landlord what rate he is going to charge on the renewal.

- **What is the deal with your security deposit?**
Perhaps when you took occupancy your business was brand new or you asked the landlord to pay for some improvements that were beyond the building standard. The landlord may do this, but they will ask for a larger security deposit than the typical month deposit. As the original lease expires, you should ask to have the security deposit returned. They might say no, but they might say yes.

SUCCESS STORIES

Below are a couple of real examples of deals I've done where we were able to save our clients lots of money! If you want to see more examples of our work follow this link: https://www.compass-commercial.com/case-studies/

Success Story One

The following case study also demonstrates that, when renewing a lease, most everything is open for negotiations.

The Challenge:

Bianchi Public Relations first approached Compass Commercial in early 2014. They'd been a tenant in the same building for 14 years and were looking for help in either renewing their lease or relocating their offices.

What We did:

Our first step was to complete a lease abstract, a full review of the lease, to help us find any business points that aren't in the client's best interest. In doing so, we uncovered several issues in the current lease, many of which were completely focused on the landlord's rights.

After doing an initial review, we identified a list of potential locations for a relocation and toured the spaces at hand. Three locations were identified as good alternatives and requests for proposals were sent out.

Upon receipt of the RFPs and review of the financials, Compass Commercial was sent to the current landlord to renegotiate the lease.

The Results:

Working with the landlord in their current space, we were able to renegotiate the terms of their current lease, reducing costs while keeping them in the same location. Upon review of their options, the communications firm decided that given the savings available to them, it made sense to stay put. Overall savings on the transaction was over $100,000 on 3,000 square feet of space, equating to a 26% reduction in rent over the term of the lease. All in all, a great end. In addition, in working with the landlord, we at Compass were able to secure the following concessions for the communications firm:

* The rental rate was reduced by 18%.
* The reduced rent would start 6 months before the original lease expiration, saving the client $8,000 in rent, immediately
* 2 free parking spaces were negotiated
* The base year for common area maintenance was reset to the current year
* The $20,000 security deposit, that was held by landlord for 14 years, was returned to the communications firm
* The landlord replaced all the flooring with upgraded carpet tiles and wood flooring, and painted the suite
* Holdover fees of 200% were reduced to 125%

- The original lease called for the landlord to have 30 days to approve a sublease and the timeline was negotiated down to 10 days (the normal timeline for this type of approval.)

Jim Bianchi
President,
Bianchi Public Relations, Inc. /
Accredited Public Relations
Professional

I highly recommend Lynn Drake if you're looking for space or considering renewing your current lease. I've worked with other agents before, but have to say that Lynn is the BEST at representing her tenant clients! She's knowledgeable, thorough and goes the extra mile to protect the interests of her clients. Although the agreement with the landlord prevents me revealing any details, let's just say I am EXTREMELY HAPPY with the deal that Lynn negotiated for me

I'm not suggesting you must move each time your lease renewal expires; all I'm asking is that you do your homework to make sure you firm is getting the best possible deal.

An interesting turn of events with this tenant is that the building went into bankruptcy within six months of renegotiating this lease. Had we not gotten the clients security deposit returned when we did it would have been lost in the bankruptcy. The building has since sold to a strong landlord and is now in a good financial situation.

Success Story Two

The Challenge:

When BSB Communications, Inc. approached Compass Commercial, they'd been a tenant in the same building for over 30 years. They had expanded into adjacent suites over the years with a mix that was 75% office space and 25% industrial. For most of that time they'd been quite happy in the space. So why leave? The floor plan was not very efficient and the building was aging.

By the time 2013 rolled around, it was also becoming apparent that the building was built on a foundation that was causing some structural issues. Thanks to business growth and concern over the structural issues, it became clear that it was time for BSB to relocate to a more suitable corporate headquarters.

BSB came to Compass Commercial looking for an alternative location. Tours were arranged and several locations in the area were considered.

THE RESULTS

After reviewing and touring several flex buildings, two were picked for final consideration. In the end, a building on Technology Park Drive won out, and for good reason:

- Rent was reduced by 12% below asking rate
- Five months of free rent were negotiated
- The landlord of the building contributed close to $40,000 in improvements for the space
- The tenant was given free furniture as an incentive to lease in the building
- The building had recently been sold and we expected the taxes to be increased significantly, which would drive up the cam charges. We therefore negotiated a 3% cap on future increases in taxes
- Expenses for replacement or repair of HVAC were capped to protect the tenant
- Tenant was granted a buyout after 5 years of the lease

Steve Klenner
Partner,
BSB Communications

WORKING WITH COMPASS COMMERCIAL

BSB prides itself on being Focused on telecommunications and leveraging our Expertise to deliver Results for our clients. We quickly realized that working with Compass Commercial and Lynn Drake, was going to produce results for BSB. As someone that focuses on tenant representation, it was clear that Lynn was representing our interests. And, her market knowledge and expertise provided us with a high degree of confidence. At all times, we felt Lynn and Compass Commercial had our back. What could have been a far more stressful process turned out to be successful move to a new location we are proud to call our new headquarters.

Success Story Three:

- **The Challenge**

A telecommunications company came to Compass Commercial with a dilemma: they had occupied the same space for close to 10 years and were on a month-to-month lease when their landlord gave them a 30 day notice to move. We had less than a month to find them a new space, negotiate a lease, and make sure they moved out in time.

Compass contacted the landlords of properties in the area who could react quickly with showings and respond to RFPs fast. Five potential locations were identified. Three RFPs were sent out for responses.

Three locations competed for our client's business including their current landlord. The property manager in their current location told our client that not including Compass Commercial in the transaction would get the client a better deal. The "deal" offered by the property manager was actually higher than the market rate for the building.

The Results

- It was determined the best option was to stay in the same building and move to another suite. The client told the landlord they would have to work with Compass Commercial and pay the customary lease fee.

- Their rental rate was reduced by $0.50 per square foot over the term of the lease

- They received six months of free rent in the new 2,500 s.f. location

- Their new landlord gave them free alternative space for 90 days while the new space was built out

- The landlord provided a turnkey buildout based upon the tenant specifications

- The telecommunications company ended up with an overall reduction of rent over the new lease term of five years of $68,000 plus a full build out paid for by the landlord.

WORKING WITH COMPASS COMMERCIAL

Ben Rife
President/CEO
Bullfrog Group, LLC

I believed our current landlords property manager when he told me he could give us a cheaper rental rate if we got rid of our Agent (Lynn Drake). However, when Lynn reviewed the numbers from the property manager we found out the offer was over market for the building. Lynn quickly renegotiated on our behalf a rental rate below what the property manager had offered. Had Lynn not been in the equation we would have over paid for the space. We were very happy with the results.

HOW TO HIRE A COMMERCIAL AGENT

If after reading all of this, you decide it is more than you want to take on and that hiring an agent is a good idea, let's talk about how best to do this.

Of course, you can always call us and we can either do the work on your behalf or find the right person to do the work for you. The article will provide you with tips on how to go about picking an agent. If you want to skip this step all together send us an email: real.estate.services@compass-commercial.com and we will find you the right agent in any market.

In the market for a new office or have some extra space available? Many people might look in the yellow pages, some will ask friends. Whichever system you use to find a realtor, make sure to screen them before hiring them.

Commercial realtors come in every shape, color, size and age. You could meet a 25-year-old and 60-year-old agent and think the older one has the experience. Don't make this mistake, the 25-year-old may not have gone to college and is now in their 7th year in the business. Conversely, the 60-year-old may have been forced from their career during the recession and has only been in the business a month.

Always ask how long the individual has been in the brokerage business.

Would you ever hire your dermatologist to deliver twins? I guess you could, but would they really understand all the intricacies involved in a complicated delivery? Just like in the medical profession, there are many types of Realtors. Each area has its own specialties.

There are residential, office, industrial, retail, land and investment realtors. These areas can be further broken down into tenant representation, buyer representation, corporate services and listing agents. Before you hire an agent make sure you are hiring the right type.

Friends of mine have asked me to list their homes, but my answer is always the same. NO! I don't have access to the residential multiple list service. How am I going to get other realtors in to see the house? While I could find out how much the houses on your street sold for, a good residential agent would know this intuitively. I'm not going to hold open houses or send flyers on your home because I don't want to develop customers in this area.

Conversely, I cringe when I see a residential agent list a commercial property. I have yet to see one list their properties in any of the commercial databases. Why, because they do not belong to them, nor do they know what they are. Occasionally, a commercial building will sell with a sign, but more likely you are going to need a specialist.

You want to hire the right agent to do the job. If you have an office building for sale or lease, don't go to a firm, which works primarily in the retail sector. They will know all the buzz terms, but will refer back up to their overseeing residential expert for an explanation. If an agent works in multiple areas, ask them questions about each area so you can assess their knowledge.

If you have a building for lease or sale, drive through the area the property is located in. Notice the agents who have lots of listings. Give them a call. Check the yellow pages and ask friends for references.

When listing a property, it is advisable to find a team – usually a junior level person combined with a senior level person. The senior person manages the account while teaching the junior level person. This gives you the advantage of two people to show the property.

The property needs to be listed in the commercial databases. The main ones being Co-star, LoopNet or the local commercial real estate multiple listing that is available in your market.

We live in a high-tech age. This can give someone a sense of an office presence when one doesn't exist. There are realtors out there who work on their own from their home. If these people get sick or take a vacation your project is at a standstill. Email, faxes and computers are essential to do business in this day and age. It is hard for me to imagine working without these basic tools but there are those trying to cut corners.

What type of advertising will the agent do for the property? The larger the property, the higher the expectations. The following are a few examples of marketing: brochures, post cards, newspaper or industry specific advertising. Find out how many pieces of mail will be sent out on this property. It is sometimes useful to find out the source for addresses.

Cold calls are not anyone's favorite thing to do, but they can bring in good results. Find out if cold calls will be made for the listing. The agent should be able to tell you whom they are targeting for prospective tenants.

Updates are essential. A good agent will keep you updated via calls and written update. Updates should include all marketing efforts including cold calls, inquiring and showings.

When hiring a realtor for an acquisition, you would ask basically the same questions. A good agent will be able to help you maneuver through some of the challenges faced when negotiating business terms. Questions about their experience and what obstacles they have overcome to reach their client's goals. For example, I always insist that my clients make offers on two sites simultaneously. That way there is more leverage while negotiating.

Interview several agents. Here are some questions you will want to ask:

Exhibit H Questions to Ask a Commercial Agent Before Hiring Them

Tenant Representative	Landlord Representative	Question
X	X	How long have you been in the real estate business?
X	X	Where are your offices?
X	X	Who fills in for you if you are on vacation or become ill?
X	X	Do you have email, cell phone and voice mail?
X	X	Do you subscribe to Co-Star?
X	X	Are you an office, industrial, retail or investment realtor?
X	X	Do you consider yourself a listing or tenant representative?
X	X	How many real estate transactions have you completed in your career?

X	X	What clients have you personally represented in the past?
X	X	Do you have a list of references?
	X	Do you work the listings alone or with a partner?
X	X	How many listings do you have?
	X	What type of marketing will you do? (flyers, advertising, email campaign etc.)
X	X	Describe what type of updates I can expect if I list the property with you.
	X	How many cold calls will make on this listing?
	X	Do you have an internet site where my listing will be featured?
	X	What websites will use to post my listing?
X	X	Why should I hire you verses the competition?
X		Do you use a written request for proposal or verbal?
X		What type of financial summaries do you provide to compare properties?

If after reading this book, you want Compass Commercial to help, we can do so in a couple of ways. First, we can act as your broker; dual agency won't be an issue. We usually spend between 20 and 40 hours on a smaller transaction and up to 100 hours on a larger transaction. We can work anywhere in North America and in some countries overseas as well.

We also have a consulting division where you can hire us for just parts of the transaction.

Thoughts to ponder while doing real estate transactions.

SUMMARY

If you go to link: http://www.compass-commercial.com/book-exhibits/ you will find downloadable PDFs on each of the exhibits in the book. There is a blank copy and one filled out to make it easier for you to follow along with the process that I use for my clients.

If we can help you with finding a space to lease or buy, finding an executive suite, if you have a commercial property you need to have listed, or help hiring an agent in your market please contact us at real.estate.services@compass-commercial.com

While we only represent tenants of office, industrial and retail space, we know who to recommend, not only in our area but also across the county.

Remember at Compass Commercial we work across North America exclusively for tenants and buyers never landlords.

To learn more about Compass Commercial visit us at our website: http://www.compass-commercial.com/ or you can contact us at real.estate.services@compass-commercial.com

Now that you can speak lease, my hope is that you found this book helpful and informative and it allowed you to complete a transaction with great results. Commercial Real Estate Costs are often in the top 5 expenses for most businesses. As a business owner myself, I know how important it is to have the best possible location and know that you didn't over pay for the space. Good luck with your site search!

Wishing you much success in your search for your firm's new business home!

Lynn Drake

Made in the USA
Monee, IL
05 November 2020